Alchemical Wisdom

Alchemistische Weisheit

Sagesse Alchimique

Pir Vilayat Inayat Khan

Original English version published by:
Sulük Press, an imprint of Omega Publications, Inc.
New Lebanon NY USA
www.omegapub.com
©2015 Omega Publications Inc., Sulük Press

Cover photograph by Martin Zamir Roehrs
Photograph of Pir Vilayat by Michael Peuckert
Layout and design by Martin Zamir Roehrs

All proceeds from the sale of this book will be donated for the development and upkeep of Fazl Manzil in Suresnes, the home of Pir Vilayat Inayat Khan and his family, the home of the Inayati Sufi Message.

Pir Vilayat Inayat Khan spoke many languages, which he mostly taught himself, so he could give his many talks and conversations in the local language. He often translated himself from English into French and German, sometimes he gave talks alternating between those three.

In this tradition, it seems appropriate to publish these sayings in one book, containing all 3 languages.

Since the first publication of these sayings in English, it has been my wish to present them in this multi language form. The year 2016 and the 100th anniversary of Pir Vilayat's birth seems the appropriate time to fulfill this wish.

Pir Vilayat Khan sprach viele Sprachen, von denen er sich viele selbst beigebracht hatte, so dass er seine vielen Vorträge und Gespräche in der jeweiligen Landessprache halten konnte. Oft übersetzte er sich selbst, vom Französichen ins Englische oder Deutsche und oft hielt er Vorträge in allen drei Sprachen.

In dieser Tradition erscheint es angemessen, diese Sprichworte in einem Buch in allen drei Sprachen gemeinsam herauszugeben. Seit die Sprichworte im Englischen erschienen sind, war es mein spontaner Wunsch, sie in dieser mehrsprachlichen Fassung zu präsentieren. Das Jahr 2016 mit dem 100. Geburtstag Pir Vilayat's erscheint als der gegebene Anlass, diesen Wunsch zu erfüllen.

Für die deutsche Übersetzung danken wir Fereshta Bechtloff und Amaité Willand, und für die gute Grundlage der ersten Übersetzung Aeostra Hamann.

Pir Vilayat Inayat Khan parlait de nombreuses langues, qu'il avait pour la plupart apprises par lui-même, afin de pouvoir donner ses enseignements et converser dans la langue du pays. Partant de l'anglais, il se traduisait souvent lui-même en français et en allemand ; il donnait parfois des exposés en alternant ces trois langues.

Suivant cette tradition, il semble approprié de publier ces citations en trois langues, dans un seul et même livre.

Depuis la publication de ces citations en anglais, j'ai souhaité les présenter sous une forme trilingue. Cette année 2016, qui marque le 100ème anniversaire de la naissance de Pir Vilayat, semble être le moment opportun pour réaliser ce souhait.

Nous tenons à remercier Uma Lacombe pour la traduction française.

Zamir Roehrs

Foreword

Pir Vilayat's retreat process was modeled on the ancient al-chemical process of transmuting lead into gold, but here it is the human heart, which, purified of its dross, reflects the divine luminosity. Often a few words, a single idea, can prove the catalyst which moves this process from one stage to the next.

These sayings are classified according to three phases of the alchemical process:

Distillation
The pure expression of a quality

Essence
The heart of a quality

Quintessence
A quality in its universal significance

The uses of the Alchemical Wisdom sayings are as wide as one's imagination. Use them as daily meditations, as reflections of your soul's purpose, as guidance in a situation. For instance, sit quietly, trusting, holding one of your challenges in your heart. Be open... Then choose a saying at random.

Put a favorite saying on your bathroom mirror, your car's dashboard, on your refrigerator. Add a quote as an inspiration in a letter to a friend. Choose a quote that is a mirror of your highest self. Share it. Then you could give it your own expression in a sound, a song, a movement or a drawing. Are you in a group that needs to make a decision? Sit quietly together and use the sayings to present a fresh perspective.

As Pir Vilayat reminds us,

Every moment is the chance of a lifetime.

Acknowledgements:

Many thanks to Arifa Miller for recording and compiling the sayings; and to Professor Donald Graham for editing and arranging the original Alchemical Wisdom cards according to stages of alchemy, for providing this foreword, and for his permission to use his work for the present version. Thanks also to Lakshmi Nancy Barta-Norton for her assistance with production work. And most of all thanks to Pir Zia Inayat-Khan for his kind permission to publish his father's sayings.

Introduction:

Following my father's [Hazrat Inayat Khan] message, I believe that to develop our being to its highest potential we need to discover our ideal and allow an inborn strength, a conviction in ourselves, to give us the courage toward developing this ideal. My deepest goal is to instill in those with whom I come into contact, a respect and tolerance for each world religion, recognizing the unity of ideals behind the diversity of forms. I believe in rising above distinctions and differences to appreciate the beauty and variety in people and cultures, and to uphold at all costs the dignity of every human being.

Pir Vilayat Inayat Khan

Avant-propos

La méthode de retraite de Pir Vilayat fut modelée sur l'ancien procédé alchimique de transmutation du plomb en or, mais au cours de la retraite, c'est le cœur humain qui, purifié de ses rebuts, reflète la luminosité divine. Bien souvent, quelques mots ou une seule idée peuvent s'avérer être un catalyseur qui fait avancer ce processus d'une étape vers une autre.

Ces citations sont classifiées selon trois phases du processus alchimique :

Distillation
L'expression pure d'une qualité

Essence
Le cœur d'une qualité

Quintessence
La signification universelle d'une qualité

L'utilisation des citations de la Sagesse Alchimique est aussi étendue que l'est votre imagination. Utilisez ces citations comme des méditations quotidiennes, comme des réflexions sur le dessein de votre âme ou comme guides dans une situation donnée. Par exemple, asseyez-vous tranquillement, en toute confiance, et considérez un de vos défis dans votre cœur. Soyez ouverts… Et puis, choisissez une des phrases au hasard.

Fixez votre citation favorite au miroir de votre salle de bains, sur le tableau de bord de votre voiture, sur votre réfrigérateur. Ajoutez une de ces citations, comme inspiration, à la lettre destinée à un ami. Choisissez une citation qui est le miroir de votre Être le plus élevé. Partagez cette citation. Puis, vous pourriez y ajouter une expression personnelle par un son, un mouvement ou un dessin. Faites-vous partie d'un groupe qui doit prendre une décision ? Alors, tous les membres du groupe peuvent se réunir et utiliser les phrases énoncées pour présenter un point de vue nouveau.

Comme nous le rappelle Pir Vilayat,

Chaque moment est la chance d'une vie.

Remerciements

Un grand merci à Arifa Miller pour avoir enregistré et compilé les citations et au professeur Donald Graham pour avoir édité et fait l'arrangement des cartes d'origine de la Sagesse Alchimique, selon les étapes alchimiques, pour avoir rédigé cet avant-propos et pour nous avoir donné la permission d'utiliser son travail pour la présente version. Merci à Lakshmi Nancy Barta-Norton pour son aide dans la production de ce travail. Et surtout, merci à Pir Vilayat Inayat-Khan pour nous avoir donné son aimable permission de publier les citations de son père.

Introduction

Faisant suite au message de mon père (Hazrat Inayat Khan), je crois que pour développer notre être jusqu'à son potentiel le plus élevé, nous avons besoin de découvrir notre idéal et de permettre à cette force innée, à cette conviction qui est en nous, de nous donner le courage d'atteindre cet idéal. Mon but le plus cher est d'instiller, en ceux avec qui j'entre en contact, le respect et la tolérance pour chaque religion et la possibilité de reconnaître l'unité des idéaux derrière la diversité des formes. Je crois qu'il est nécessaire de s'élever au-delà des distinctions et des différences afin d'apprécier la beauté et la diversité dans les êtres et dans les cultures, et d'affirmer à tout prix la dignité en chaque être humain.

Pir Vilayat Inayat Khan

Vorwort

Pir Vilayats Retreatprozess hat sein Vorbild im historischen alchemistischen Prozess, durch dem Blei in Gold verwandelt wird. Hier ist es aber das menschliche Herz welches, befreit von seinen Schlacken, das göttliche Leuchten widerspiegelt. Oft sind es nur ein paar Worte, eine einzige Idee, die sich als Katalysator erweisen, um den Prozess von einem Stadium in das nächste zu führen.

Diese Sätze wurden drei verschieden Phasen des alchemistischen Prozesses zugeordnet:

Destillation
Der reine Ausdruck einer Qualität

Essenz
Das Herz einer Qualität

Quintessenz
Eine Qualität in ihrer universellen Bedeutung

Die Möglichkeiten für den Einsatz der Alchemistischen Weisheitssätze sind so groß, wie die Vorstellungskraft es erlaubt. Verwenden Sie sie als tägliche Meditationen, als Reflektionen über die Bestimmung Ihrer Seele oder als Führung in einer Situation.

Sie können zum Beispiel still sitzen, ins Vertrauen gehen und dann eine ihrer Herausforderungen in ihrem Herzen halten. Seien Sie offen...

und dann wählen Sie zufällig einen Satz.

Befestigen Sie einen Lieblingssatz an Ihrem Badezimmerspiegel, am Armaturenbrett Ihres Autos oder an Ihrem Kühlschrank. Fügen Sie ein Zitat dem Brief an einen Freund als Inspiration bei. Wählen Sie ein Zitat, das Ihr höchstes Selbst widerspiegelt. Erzählen Sie es anderen. Ausserdem könnten Sie ihm auch einen ganz eigenen Ausdruck verleihen – in einem Klang, einem Lied, einer Bewegung oder einer Zeichnung. Sind Sie in einer Gruppe, die eine Entscheidung fällen muss? Sitzen Sie still zusammen und nuzten Sie die Sätze, um eine neue Perspektive zu bekommen.

Wie Pir Vilayat uns erinnert:

Jeder Augenblick ist die Chance ihres Lebens.

Danksagungen:

Vielen Dank an Arifa Miller, die diese Zitate aufschrieb und zusammenstellte; und an Professor Donald Graham, der sie editierte, die ursprünglichen Alchemistischen Weisheitskarten gemäß der Stufen in der Alchemie ordnete und der dieses Vorwort schrieb; und auch für seine Erlaubnis, seine Arbeit für die hier vorliegende Version zu verwenden. Dank auch an Lakshmi Nancy Barta-Norton für ihre Hilfe bei der Herstellung des ursprünglichen Kartensets. Vor allem geht der Dank aber an Pir Zia Inayat Khan für seine freundliche Genehmigung, die Sinnsprüche seines Vaters zu veröffentlichen.

Einführung:

Entsprechend der Botschaft meines Vaters (Hazrat Inayat-Khan) glaube ich, dass wir, um das höchste Potential unseres Wesens zu entfalten, unser Ideal entdecken müssen, und wir unserer angeborenen Stärke, einer inneren Überzeugung, ermöglichen müssen, uns den Mut zu verleihen, dieses Ideal auszubilden. Mein höchstes Ziel ist allen, denen ich begegne, Respekt und Toleranz für jede Religion einzuflößen, indem wir die Einheit der Ideale hinter der Vielfalt der Formen erkennen. Ich glaube daran, sich über die Trennungen und Unterschiede zu erheben, um die Schönheit und Vielfalt der Völker und Kulturen zu würdigen, und unter allen Umständen die Würde jedes Menschen zu wahren.

Pir Vilayat Inayat Khan

Destillation

Unless we awaken them, our capacities will always
lie dormant.

> Unsere Fähigkeiten werden solange schlummern,
> bis wir sie erwecken.

A moins de les réveiller, nos facultés resteront
dormantes.

As long as you are convinced of your opinion, you
will not rely upon your intuition.

> So lange Sie von Ihrer Meinung überzeugt sind,
> werden Sie sich nicht auf Ihre Intuition verlassen.

Tant que vous tenez à vos opinions vous ne pouvez pas vous fier à votre intuition.

The mantra for freedom from opinion is,
"What if?"

> Das Mantra für Freiheit von Meinungen ist
> „What if?" („Was wäre, wenn?")

Le mantra pour la liberté d'opinion est
« Qu'en serait-il si ? »

Base your being on a master, but be creative.

> Stützen Sie Ihr Wesen auf einen Meister, aber seien Sie kreativ.

Basez votre être sur celui d'un maître, mais soyez créatifs.

See how your involvement affects your freedom.

> Beobachten Sie, wie Ihr Engagement sich auf Ihre Freiheit auswirkt.

Voyez comme votre engagement affecte votre volonté.

We foster ecstasy by not being fooled by appearances and rising to splendor.

> Wir begünstigen Ekstase, indem wir uns nicht von den Erscheinungen täuschen lassen und uns zur Herrlichkeit aufschwingen.

Nous favorisons l'extase en ne nous laissant pas berner par les apparences et en nous élevant vers la splendeur.

The ultimate help to others is to help them help themselves.

> Die beste Hilfe für andere ist ihnen zu helfen, sich selbst zu helfen.

La meilleure aide que l'on puisse offrir aux autres c'est de les aider à s'aider eux-mêmes.

Guilt and resentment are two causes for lack of joy.

> Schuldgefühle und Groll sind zwei Gründe für einen Mangel an Freude.

La culpabilité et le ressentiment sont deux causes du manque de joie.

"Turn the other cheek" is absolutely irrational, but makes the ultimate sense.

> "Halte die andere Wange hin" ist völlig irrational, aber es macht den letztendlichen Sinn aus.

„Tendre l'autre joue » est tout à fait irrationnel, mais c'est finalement tout à fait sensé.

Do not pride yourself on humility or poverty;
pride yourself on your divine inheritance.

> Seien Sie nicht stolz auf Ihre Bescheidenheit oder
> Armut; seien Sie stolz auf Ihre göttliche Erbschaft.

Ne soyez pas fiers de votre humilité ou de votre
pauvreté ; soyez fiers de votre héritage divin.

Meditation is for those who don't love enough.

> Meditation ist für diejenigen, die nicht genug
> lieben.

La méditation est pour ceux qui n'aiment pas
assez.

Let yourself reach into the inner space where you
have contact with all beings.

> Gewähren Sie sich selbst Zugang zu dem inneren
> Raum, wo Sie Kontakt zu allen Wesen haben.

Allez atteindre l'espace intérieur dans lequel vous
êtes en relation avec tous les êtres.

Spiritual practices are planting seeds in the sub-
conscious, which will eventually bear fruit.

Spirituelle Übungen sähen Samen in das Unterbe-
wusstsein, die eines Tages Früchte tragen werden.

Les pratiques spirituelles sont comme des graines
que l'on planterait dans le subconscient et qui, un
jour, porteront des fruits.

We are all handicapped by our personal identity.

Wir sind alle durch unsere persönliche Identität
eingeschränkt.

Nous sommes tous handicapés par notre identité
personnelle.

It's a discipline of mind to see beauty in ugliness.

Es ist eine Wissenschaft des Geistes, Schönheit im
Hässlichen zu sehen.

Voir la beauté dans la laideur est une discipline du
mental.

The power of detachment is the power of silence,
of peace.

> Die Macht der Losgelöstheit ist die Macht der
> Stille, des Friedens.

La puissance du détachement est la puissance du
silence, de la paix.

You can't be creative through will. You must be in
a state where you need to create.

> Man kann nicht willentlich kreativ sein. Man
> muss in einem Zustand sein, in dem man schöp-
> ferisch sein muss.

Vous ne pouvez pas être créatifs par la force de la
volonté ; vous devez être dans un état dans lequel
créer est un besoin.

Don't be concerned about being disloyal to your
pain by being joyous.

> Machen Sie sich keine Sorgen, Ihrem Schmerz
> untreu zu werden, wenn Sie voller Freude sind.

Ne vous souciez pas d'être déloyaux envers votre
peine lorsque vous êtes joyeux.

The mind is a wonderful instrument of justification.

> Der Verstand ist ein wunderbares Instrument für Rechtfertigungen.

Le mental est un merveilleux instrument de justification.

You can only help someone if you know their problem yourself: you have been through it and somehow you managed to find freedom.

> Sie können einem anderen nur helfen, wenn Sie sein Problem selbst kennen: Sie sind hindurchgegangen und haben es irgendwie geschafft, Freiheit zu erlangen.

Vous ne pouvez aider autrui que si vous connaissez son problème pour l'avoir vous-mêmes vécu, et pour avoir pu vous en rendre libre, d'une manière ou d'une autre.

One needs something to trigger off one's attunement instead of one's thinking.

> Wir brauchen etwas, das unsere Einstimmung an-
> regt statt unser Denken.

On a besoin de quelque chose qui suscite l'harmonie plutôt que la pensée.

You have to get yourself into a deep state of consciousness to be able to rely on your intuition;
judgement is not reliable.

> Man muss in einen tiefen Bewusstseinszustand
> kommen, um sich auf seine Intuition verlassen zu
> können; das Urteilsvermögen ist nicht verlässlich.

Vous devez atteindre un état de conscience pro-
fond afin de pouvoir vous fier à votre intuition; le
jugement n'est pas fiable.

A little prayer on earth can ignite an enormous
cosmic celebration.

> Ein kleines Gebet auf der Erde kann eine gewalti-
> ge kosmische Feier entfachen.

Une petite prière sur terre peut déclencher une
immense célébration cosmique.

By accepting one's own shadow one gives unconditional love to all beings.

> Indem man seinen eigenen Schatten annimmt,
> schenkt man allen Wesen bedingungslose Liebe.

C'est en acceptant ses propres ombres que l'on
porte un amour inconditionnel à tous les êtres.

If you seek for happiness it will escape you; like a
bird in the forest, the more you chase it, the far-
ther it will evade your grasp.

> Wenn Sie das Glück suchen, wird es Ihnen ent-
> fliehen wie ein Vogel im Wald: je mehr Sie ihm
> nachjagen, desto weiter wird es sich Ihrem Zugriff
> entziehen.

Si vous cherchez le bonheur, il vous échappera.
C'est comme un oiseau dans la forêt : plus vous le
chassez plus il s'envole loin de votre prise.

Consider every situation which causes pain to your heart as the way in which life strikes this living receptacle to make it vibrant, radiant, alive, sensitive.

> Betrachten Sie jede Situation, die Ihrem Herzen Schmerz bereitet, als die Art, wie das Leben dieses lebendige Gefäß anschlägt, um es pulsierend, strahlend, lebendig und sensibel zu machen.

Considérez chaque situation qui cause de la peine à votre cœur comme étant la façon dans laquelle la vie frappe ce réceptacle vivant afin de la rendre vibrant, radieux, vivant et sensible.

There's no such thing as inanimate matter; everything is a being.

> So etwas wie unbelebte Materie gibt es nicht; alle Dinge sind Lebewesen.

La matière ne peut pas être inanimée ; tout est vivant.

The whole universe is breathing as our breath; we
limit the process by our assumption that we are
doing the breathing.

> Das ganze Universum atmet als unser Atem; wir
> begrenzen diesen Vorgang durch unsere Annah-
> me, dass wir es sind, die atmen.

L'univers entier respire dans notre souffle ; nous
limitons le processus quand nous présumons que
c'est nous qui respirons.

Overcome resentment against people and against
God.

> Überwinden Sie den Groll gegen Menschen und
> gegen Gott.

Surmontez votre ressentiment envers les êtres ainsi qu'envers Dieu.

Music helps us bypass the mind.

> Musik hilft uns, den Verstand zu umgehen.

La musique nous apprend à contourner le mental.

Meditation is about learning how to optimize the potentialities of our being.

> In der Meditation geht es darum zu lernen, die Potentiale unseres Wesens zu optimieren.

La méditation c'est apprendre comment faire pour optimiser les potentialités de notre être.

Anger is our defense system.

> Ärger ist unser Abwehrsystem.

La colère est notre système de défense.

We can learn to put pain to good use. This is the great art: to capitalize on pain, using it as a catalyst to enhance inspiration.

> Wir können lernen, Schmerz sinnvoll zu nutzen. Das ist die große Kunst: aus dem Schmerz Nutzen zu ziehen, indem wir ihn als Katalysator verwenden, um die Inspiration zu steigern.

Nous pouvons apprendre à bien utiliser la peine. Ceci est le grand art : tirer parti de la peine, l'utiliser comme catalyseur afin d'augmenter l'inspiration.

The sense of sacredness triggers off self-valida-
tion, which in turn permits personal creativity.

Der Sinn für das Heilige führt zur Wertschätzung
des Selbst, was wiederum persönliche Kreativität
ermöglicht.

Le sens du sacré suscite la confirmation de la va-
leur de notre être, ce qui, à son tour, permet la
créativité personnelle.

Spirituality is a tonic for the injured psyche rather
than a sedative, because the act of glorification un-
veils the divine status of one's own being.

Spiritualität ist für die verletzte Psyche eher ein
Stärkungs- als ein Beruhigungsmittel, weil der Akt
der Verherrlichung den göttlichen Zustand des eigenen Wesens enthüllt.

La spiritualité est un tonique, plutôt qu'un sédatif
pour la psyché blessée, parce que l'acte de glorification dévoile le statut divin de notre être.

At every move our intentions are tested, tested by
life itself.

> Bei jedem unserer Schritte wird unsere Absicht
> geprüft, geprüft durch das Leben selbst.

Nos intentions sont vérifiées lors de chaque
action; c'est la vie même qui les vérifie.

There is the despair of not having what one wants,
and that is pain; pain is the first call of every heart.

> Die Verzweiflung darüber, nicht zu bekommen,
> was man will, ist Schmerz. Schmerz ist für jedes
> Herz der erste Weckruf.

Eprouver du désespoir lorsque l'on n'obtient pas ce
que l'on veut engendre la peine ; la peine est le premier appel de chaque cœur.

You are sharing in the totality of cosmic pain. You are called upon to meet it in joy instead of succumbing to self-pity.

> Sie nehmen an der Gesamtheit des kosmischen Schmerzes teil. Sie sind dazu aufgerufen, dem in Freude zu begegnen, anstatt in Selbstmitleid zu verfallen.

Vous partagez la totalité de la souffrance cosmique. Il vous est demandé d'y faire face avec joie plutôt que de succomber à la pitié pour vous-mêmes.

See if you can get an answer to your heart's greatest longing by knocking upon the door of your heart.

> Klopfen Sie an die Tür Ihres Herzens, um Antwort auf die größte Sehnsucht Ihres Herzens zu bekommen.

Voyez si vous pouvez obtenir une réponse au plus grand désir de votre cœur en frappant à la porte de ce dernier.

Think of God as an artist who keeps changing His/Her mind.

> Stellen Sie sich Gott als einen Künstler vor, der ständig Ihre/Seine Meinung ändert.

Imaginez Dieu comme étant un artiste qui changerait sans cesse d'avis.

What life is telling us is to find freedom.

> Das Leben fordert uns dazu auf, Freiheit zu finden.

La vie nous pousse à trouver la liberté.

We can create four conditions to be favorable to the revelation of the Divine Intention: with Silence, Solitude, Fasting, and Watchfulness.

> Wir können vier begünstigende Bedingungen für die Offenbarung der göttlichen Absicht schaffen: Stille, Einsamkeit, Fasten und Achtsamkeit.

Nous pouvons créer quatre conditions favorables à la révélation de l'Intention divine : le Silence, la Solitude, le Jeûne, la Vigilance.

All creativity starts with attunement and that attunement finds its way into form.

Alle Kreativität beginnt mit Einstimmung, und diese Einstimmung findet ihren Weg in die Form.

Toute créativité commence dans l'harmonie ; c'est en fait l'harmonie qui cherche à prendre forme.

Laughing at your own stupidity is the first step toward sanity.

Über seine eigene Dummheit zu lachen ist der erste Schritt zu geistiger Gesundheit.

Rire de sa propre bêtise est le premier pas vers la santé de l'esprit.

Some people bring out the worst in us, and perhaps that is good.

Manche Menschen bringen das Schlimmste in uns zum Vorschein, und vielleicht ist das gut.

Certaines personnes font ressortir nos pires défauts ; cela est peut-être une bonne chose.

Physicists are now studying the way glorification manifests as the wish to reach the throne of God.

> Die Physiker untersuchen jetzt, wie sich Verherrlichung als Wunsch zeigt, den göttlichen Thron zur erreichen.

De nos jours, les physiciens étudient comment la glorification se manifeste dans le souhait d'atteindre le trône de Dieu.

You were born out of an act of glory, and when you have found your being, you can suddenly be transformed.

> Sie wurden aus Verherrlichung heraus geboren, und wenn Sie Ihr wahres Wesen gefunden haben, können Sie in einem Augenblick transformiert werden.

Vous êtes nés grâce à un acte de glorification et lorsque vous vous trouvez vous-mêmes, vous pouvez être soudainement transformé.

Cosmic programming can't predict everything;
otherwise there is no progress. The future is not
entirely predictable.

> Die kosmische Programmierung kann nicht
> alles vorherbestimmen, sonst gäbe es keinen
> Fortschritt. Die Zukunft ist nicht vollständig
> vorhersehbar.

La programmation cosmique ne prédit pas tout ;
sinon il n'y aurait pas de progrès. L'avenir ne peut
être entièrement prédit.

Does one have the strength to scan one's heart to
provide excuses for those who have betrayed one's
love?

> Haben wir die Stärke, in unserem Herzen nach
> Entschuldigungen für jene zu suchen, die unsere
> Liebe verraten haben?

Avons-nous la force de scruter notre cœur afin
d'y trouver des excuses à ceux qui ont trahi notre
amour?

Love transforms you from death into life: it quickens you to be able to see where you cannot see and feel where you cannot feel.

> Liebe verwandelt Tod in Leben: sie belebt uns, damit wir fähig sind zu sehen, wo wir nicht sehen können und fühlen, wo wir nicht fühlen können.

L'amour vous fait passer de la mort à la vie : il vous active afin que vous puissiez voir là où vous ne pouviez pas voir et sentir là où vous ne pouviez pas sentir.

Meditation can very easily become an ego trip, and the only way to avoid this is to preserve the dimension of glorification in meditation.

> Meditation kann sehr leicht zum Egotrip werden, und dies kann man nur vermeiden, indem man in der Meditation die Dimension der Verherrlichung bewahrt.

La méditation peut facilement devenir un exercice d'autosatisfaction ; la seule façon d'éviter cela est de préserver la dimension de glorification dans la méditation.

A crystal is an expression of glory, a prayer which
has become petrified emotion.

> **Ein** Kristall ist ein Ausdruck der Verherrlichung,
> zu Stein gewordene Emotion eines Gebets.

Le cristal est une expression de la gloire, une
prière devenue émotion pétrifiée.

The greatest help in giving expression to the depth
which we never express in our everyday life is to
get into the consciousness of a master, saint, a
prophet.

> **Die** größte Hilfe dabei, der Tiefe einen Ausdruck
> zu verleihen, die wir im Alltag niemals ausdrü-
> cken, besteht darin, in das Bewusstsein eines
> Meisters, Heiligen oder Propheten einzutreten.

Entrer dans la conscience d'un maître, d'un saint
ou d'un prophète nous aidera grandement à exprimer cette profondeur en nous, qui jamais ne s'exprime dans la vie quotidienne.

One cannot "should" oneself, or another person,
to be a hero. But giving vent to the latent hero in
one is a great fulfillment.

> Weder man selbst noch jemand anderes kann ein
> Held „sein sollen", aber dem verborgenen Helden
> in sich Raum zu geben, ist sehr erfüllend.

On ne peut pas se forcer, ni forcer autrui, à être un
héros. Mais donner libre cours à son héros intérieur latent est une grande réalisation.

Resentment can degenerate into hatred, but it can
be transmuted by heroism.

> Ärger kann in Hass ausarten, aber durch Helden-
> tum kann er verwandelt werden.

Le ressentiment peut dégénérer en haine, mais il
peut être transmuté par l'héroïsme.

Pain is as frost is to some plants: it strengthens them. Pain is very important in the transformation of a person.

> Schmerz ist wie Frost für manche Pflanzen: Er kräftigt sie. Schmerz ist für die Transformation eines Menschen sehr wichtig.

La douleur est ce qu'est la gelée à certaines plantes : elle leur donne de la force. La douleur est très importante dans la transformation d'une personne.

If we are indeed the convergence of the universe at all levels, we are those spheres which we think are out of our reach.

> Wenn wir tatsächlich der Ort der Vereinigung aller Ebenen des Universums sind, dann sind wir auch jene Sphären, von denen wir annehmen, dass sie außerhalb unserer Reichweite seien.

Si nous sommes bien la convergence de l'univers sur tous les plans, nous sommes aussi ces sphères que nous pensons être hors de portée.

The human spirit lives on creativity and dies in conformity and routine.

> Der menschliche Geist lebt von Kreativität und stirbt an Gleichförmigkeit und Routine.

L'esprit humain vit de la créativité et meurt de la conformité et de la routine.

Instead of asking oneself, "What do I need to do to be successful?" ask "Am I being true to myself?"

> Anstatt sich zu fragen, "Was muss ich tun, um erfolgreich zu sein?", fragen Sie sich: „Bin ich mir selbst treu?"

Au lieu de se demander : "Que dois-je faire pour réussir?" demandons-nous plutôt "Suis-je sincère avec moi-même?"

Creativity is discovering possibilities that have not yet manifested in the universe by actuating them.

> Kreativität bedeutet, Möglichkeiten zu entdecken, die im Universum noch nicht manifest sind, indem man sie verwirklicht.

La créativité consiste à découvrir les possibilités non encore manifestées dans l'univers, dans le temps même qu'on les réalise.

The same pain that can blemish our personality
can act as a creative force, burnishing it into an
object of delight.

> Der gleiche Schmerz, der unsere Persönlichkeit
> entstellen kann, kann auch als schöpferische Kraft
> wirken, die sie poliert und zum Leuchten bringt.

La même souffrance qui peut ternir notre personnalité peut agir comme force créatrice, qui la polit
pour en faire un objet exquis.

If human beings did not think they depended
upon God, they would become monsters (and
they do).

> Wenn die Menschen nicht denken würden, sie
> seien abhängig von Gott, würden sie zu Monstern
> werden (und das tun sie).

Si les êtres humains ne pensaient pas dépendre de
Dieu, ils deviendraient des monstres (et c'est bien
ce qui se passe).

The whole meaning of prayer is that one has to ask
for something from God; one can't imagine that
one can just do everything oneself.

> Die eigentliche Bedeutung des Gebetes ist, dass
> man Gott um etwas bitten muss. Man kann nicht
> glauben, dass man alles einfach selber machen
> kann.

Tout le sens de la prière réside dans le fait que
l'on demande quelque chose à Dieu ; on ne saurait
s'imaginer être capables de tout faire soi-même.

An uncompromising person is not balanced.

> Eine unnachgiebige Person ist nicht ausgeglichen.

Une personne inflexible n'est pas équilibrée.

Unless one is prepared to restructure, one is not
part of the evolutionary process.

> Solange man nicht bereit ist, sich neu zu struk-
> turieren, nimmt man nicht am Evolutionsprozess
> teil.

Tant que l'on n'est pas prêt à se restructurer, on ne
saurait participer au procédé d'évolution.

When there is unconditional love, one does not
need to find an alibi for any person's behaviour.

> Wer bedingungslos liebt, braucht nicht nach einer
> Entschuldigung für das Verhalten von irgend je-
> mandem zu suchen.

Lorsqu'il y a amour inconditionnel, il n'est pas besoin de chercher des excuses au comportement
d'autrui.

Think of all those whose hearts you have quick-
ened: embrace them with your being.

> Denken Sie an all jene, deren Herzen Sie beflügelt
> haben: Umarmen Sie sie mit Ihrem Wesen.

Pensez à tous ceux dont vous avez réveillé le cœur:
enlacez-les de votre être.

There is no point in doing any meditation until every little bit of grudge against any being has been completely uprooted.

> Es macht keinen Sinn zu meditieren, solange nicht jedes kleinste bisschen Groll gegen irgendein anderes Lebewesen vollständig ausgemerzt ist.

Il est vain de méditer tant que le moindre ressentiment envers un être n'a pas été complètement déraciné.

The Tibetans say that the body is a wonderful instrument in which to promote illumination, providing one knows how to transform bodily functions.

> Die Tibeter sagen, dass der Körper ein wunderbares Instrument ist, um Erleuchtung zu erlangen, vorausgesetzt, man weiß, wie man Körperfunktionen transformiert.

D'après les Tibétains, le corps est un merveilleux instrument pour favoriser l'illumination, pourvu que l'on sache transformer les fonctions corporelles.

Extend the walls of your personal image to include
more of the dimensions of your divinity.

> Erweitern Sie die Grenzen Ihres Selbstbildes, um
> weitere Dimensionen Ihrer Göttlichkeit miteinzu-
> beziehen.

Repoussez les murs de l'image que vous avez de
vous afin d'y inclure un peu plus de votre dimension divine.

You can meet resentment by finding room in your
heart for the one who has offended you.

> Sie können Ihrem Ärger begegnen, indem sie für
> denjenigen, der Sie verletzt hat, in Ihrem Herzen
> Raum finden.

Vous pouvez faire face au ressentiment en faisant
de la place, dans votre coeur, pour celui qui vous a
offensé.

The Sufis say, "You have been invited to the divine banquet, and here you are crawling after crumbs."

> Die Sufis sagen, "Du wurdest zum göttlichen Festmahl eingeladen, und hier bist du nun und bückst dich nach Krümeln."

Les soufis disent : « Vous avez été invités au banquet divin et vous voilà à ramper pour quelques miettes. »

Detachment keeps you from being trapped.

> Loslösung bewahrt Sie davor, sich vereinnahmen zu lassen.

Le détachement vous évite d'être piégés.

The shadows of the world rob the soul of the vision of light.

> Die Schatten der Welt rauben der Seele die Fähigkeit, das Licht zu sehen.

Les ombres du monde dérobent à l'âme la vision de la lumière.

By giving form through imagination - vagabond-
ing in realms of light - we become both spectator
and participant.

Indem wir durch unsere Vorstellungskraft Formen schaffen - in Lichtwelten umherschweifend
- werden wir sowohl zum Zuschauer als auch zum
Teilnehmer.

En donnant forme par l'imagination (en vagabon-
dant dans les royaumes de lumière), nous deve-
nons spectateurs et participants.

There can be progress only by shattering your understanding to allow a greater understanding to
come through.

Fortschritt geschieht nur durch die Erschütterung
unseres Verständnisses, damit ein größeres Verständnis durchbrechen kann.

Il ne peut y avoir progrès qu'en ébranlant notre
compréhension, afin de permettre à une plus
grande compréhension de poindre.

Our personality threads through the consciousness of all beings and is the convergence of the
consciousness of all beings.

Unsere Persönlichkeit webt sich durch das Bewusstsein aller Wesen und fließt in dem Bewusstsein aller Wesen zusammen.

Notre personnalité pénètre la conscience de tous
les êtres et est aussi le point de convergence de la
conscience de tous les êtres.

There are no limits to your being, only those you
ascribe to yourself.

Ihr Wesen hat keine Beschränkungen außer denen, die Sie sich selbst zuschreiben.

Il n'y a pas de limites à votre être, seulement celles
que vous vous imposez.

Our creativity is programming, creating the software of the universe.

> Unsere Kreativität bedeutet Programmieren, das heißt die Software des Universums zu gestalten.

Notre créativité est dans le fait de programmer et de créer les logiciels de l'univers.

One source of power is being very deeply moved by the marvel of the universe.

> Eine Kraftquelle besteht darin, durch das Wunder des Universums zutiefst bewegt zu sein.

Une des sources de la puissance est le fait d'être profondément touché par cette merveille qu'est l'univers.

Listen to the secret language of nature.

> Lauschen Sie der geheimen Sprache der Natur.

Ecoutez le langage secret de la nature.

If you neglect something, it falls out of your control.

> Wenn Sie etwas vernachlässigen, entgleitet es ihrer Kontrolle.

Si vous négligez quelque chose, cette chose échappera à votre contrôle.

One is only ready to be a teacher if one doesn't want to be a teacher.

> Man ist nur fähig, ein Lehrer zu sein, wenn man kein Lehrer sein möchte.

On est prêt à enseigner si l'on ne désire pas être enseignant.

Put your soul in charge of your life.

> Übertragen Sie Ihrer Seele die Verantwortung für Ihr Leben.

Confiez à votre âme la responsabilité de votre vie.

It is impossible to transmute suffering into joy
without loving.

> Ohne zu lieben ist es unmöglich, Leid in Freude
> zu wandeln.

Sans amour, il est impossible de transformer la
souffrance en joie.

The only veil that separates this world from the
other world is our mind.

> Unser Denken ist der einzige Schleier, der diese
> Welt von jener Welt trennt.

Le seul voile qui sépare ce monde de l'autre
monde, c'est notre mental.

Our thinking must be in harmony with the thinking of the universe to be valid.

> Unser Denken muss mit dem Denken des Univer-
> sums in Harmonie sein, um wirksam zu sein.

Pour être valable, notre pensée doit être en harmonie avec la pensée de l'univers.

In dealing with an ugly situation beautifully, one is creating circumstances to develop the divinity of one's being.

> Wenn man mit einer hässlichen Situation schön umgeht, erschafft man Umstände, in denen sich die Göttlichkeit des eigenen Wesens entfalten kann.

Lorsque l'on traite une vilaine situation de belle manière, on créer les circonstances nécessaires au développement de la divinité en soi.

We need to be uplifted by an act of glorification.

> Wir müssen durch einen Akt der Verherrlichung erhoben werden.

Nous avons besoin d'être élevés par un acte de glorification.

It is impossible to radiate light if one is harboring resentment or guilt.

> Es ist unmöglich Licht auszustrahlen, wenn man Groll oder Schuldgefühle hegt.

Il est impossible de rayonner de la lumière si l'on garde du resssentiment ou de la culpabilité.

Every moment is the chance of a lifetime.

> Jeder Augenblick ist die Chance ihres Lebens.

Chaque instant est la chance d'une vie.

We don't know what to do with our freedom.

> Wir wissen nichts mit unserer Freiheit anzufangen.

Nous ne savons que faire de notre liberté.

Instead of complaining, see if there is not some
sense in what is happening.

> Anstatt zu klagen, prüfen Sie, ob das, was ge-
> schieht, nicht doch irgendwie Sinn macht.

Au lieu de vous plaindre, voyez si ce qui arrive n'a
pas une signification.

That which seemed a problem often avers itself to
be the best thing that could have happened to you.

> Oft erweist sich das, was zunächst als Problem er-
> schien, als das Beste, was einem passieren konnte.

Ce qui semblait être un problème s'avère être souvent comme la meilleure chose qui ait pu vous
arriver.

Grace is the greatest gift: no limitation, a blank
check.

> Gnade ist das größte Geschenk: keine Begren-
> zung, ein Blankoscheck.

La grâce est le plus grand des dons : elle est sans
limite, comme un chèque en blanc.

To bring the sublime into the mundane is the
greatest challenge there is.

> Das Erhabene in das Weltliche zu bringen ist die
> größte Herausforderung, die es gibt.

Apporter le sublime dans ce qui est mondain est le
plus grand défi qui soit.

The Sufis wish for the body to participate in the experience of the soul.

> Die Sufis wollen, dass der Körper an der Erfahrung der Seele teilhat.

Les soufis souhaitent que le corps participe à l'expérience de l'âme.

If you dedicate yourself to service, the doors will open.

> Wenn Sie sich in Dienst stellen, werden sich die Türen öffnen.

Si vous vous vouez à servir, des portes vont s'ouvrir.

In our relationships we need to uphold that aspect
of the person which is the real person and the soul
beyond their own self-doubt.

Wir müssen in unseren Beziehungen den Aspekt
eines Menschen achten, der das wahre Wesen und
die Seele jenseits seiner eigenen Selbstzweifel ist.

Dans nos relations, nous devons mettre en avant
cet aspect d'une personne qui exprime son être
réel et son âme, au-delà de ses doutes.

We are always trying to avoid a crisis, so we pro-
crastinate. But the only way to avoid sclerosis is to
go ahead and have the crisis.

Wir versuchen immer, Krisen zu vermeiden, und
so zögern wir. Aber der einzige Weg Verhärtung
zu vermeiden, ist vorwärts zu gehen und die Krise
zuzulassen.

Nous cherchons toujours à éviter une crise en la
repoussant à plus tard. Mais la seule manière d'éviter la sclérose c'est d'aller de l'avant en faisant face
à la crise.

False humility is an inverted form of pride.

>Falsche Bescheidenheit ist eine umgekehrte Form von Stolz.

La fausse humilité est une forme d'orgueil.

Is someone hurting you? Feel their suffering.

>Verletzt Sie jemand? Fühlen Sie deren Leid.

Quelqu'un vous blesse-t-il ? Ressentez sa souffrance.

The more freedom there is in a marriage, the less need there is for compromises.

>Je mehr Freiheit in einer Ehe besteht, desto weniger sind Kompromisse notwendig.

Plus il y a de liberté dans un mariage, moins les compromis sont nécessaires.

You cannot always control your mind, but you can
give it direction.

> Sie können Ihr Denken nicht immer kontrollie-
> ren, aber Sie können ihm Richtung geben.

Vous ne pouvez pas toujours contrôler votre
mental mais vous pouvez lui donner une ligne
directrice.

Cast the light from your eyes on a star; in light-
years of time, the star receives your light.

> Richten Sie das Licht Ihrer Augen auf einen
> Stern; Lichtjahre später wird der Stern Ihr Licht
> empfangen.

Portez la lumière de vos yeux sur une étoile et, des
années-lumière plus tard, l'étoile reçoit votre lumière.

Do not entertain guilt that is not justified.

> Hegen Sie keine Schuldgefühle, die nicht gerecht-
> fertigt sind.

N'entretenez pas une culpabilité qui n'est pas
justifiée.

Be very truthful about resentment. Are we ready
to forgive? We have to accept it if we are not ready.

> Seien Sie sehr wahrhaftig im Umgang mit Groll.
> Sind wir bereit zu vergeben? Wir müssen akzep-
> tieren, wenn wir dazu nicht bereit sind.

Soyons très sincères quant au ressentiment.
Sommes-nous prêts à pardonner ? Si nous ne
sommes pas prêts nous devons accepter ce fait.

If we just simply react to the challenge of life, we
are not using all the resourcefulness in our being.

> Wenn wir auf die Herausforderungen des Lebens
> einfach nur reagieren, nutzen wir nicht das ge-
> samte Potential unseres Wesens.

Si nous ne faisons que réagir au défi de la vie nous
n'utilisons pas toutes les ressources de notre être.

In the beginning of creativity there is not just the personal emotion but the emotion of the universe.

Am Anfang der Kreativität steht nicht nur die persönliche Emotion, sondern auch die Emotion des Universums.

Au commencement de la créativité, il n'y a pas seulement l'émotion personnelle mais aussi l'émotion de l'univers.

A crisis can be good; we unfold in a crisis, and we are forced to make a decision, for better or worse.

Eine Krise kann gut sein: Wir entfalten uns in einer Krise, und wir sind wohl oder übel gezwungen, eine Entscheidung zu treffen.

Une crise peut avoir du bon ; nous nous dévoilons en période de crise et nous sommes forcés de prendre une décision pour le meilleur ou pour le pire.

For the sake of honesty we have to avoid sanc-
timoniousness. We can then convey truth with
integrity.

Um der Redlichkeit willen müssen wir Scheinhei-
ligkeit vermeiden. So können wir Wahrheit mit
Integrität vermitteln.

Par honnêteté nous devons éviter d'être moralisa-
teurs ; ainsi pourrons-nous transmettre la vérité
avec intégrité.

All creativity is a fluctuation against static order-
liness.

Alle Kreativität ist eine Bewegung gegen statische
Ordnung.

Toute créativité est une fluctuation de l'ordre
statique.

Everyone is in life according to his realization, and that is what meditation is about: increasing realization.

> Alle stehen im Leben entsprechend ihrer Erkenntnis, und darum geht es in der Meditation: diese Erkenntnis zu erweitern.

Chacun vit à la hauteur de sa réalisation personnelle, et le but de la méditation est d'accroître cette réalisation.

Have the courage to manifest who you are without taking refuge in false humility.

> Haben Sie den Mut zu sein, wer Sie sind, ohne in falsche Bescheidenheit zu flüchten.

Ayez le courage de manifester qui vous êtes sans vous réfugier dans la fausse humilité.

Think in terms of resonance instead of concepts,
facts, pigeon holes.

> Denken Sie im Sinne von Resonanz anstatt von
> Konzepten, Fakten und Schubladen.

Pensez dans le sens d'une résonnance plutôt que
sous forme de concepts, de faits et de pensées
toutes faites

Do not pay attention to clues when you want to go
by your intuition.

> Achten Sie nicht auf Zeichen, wenn Sie sich nach
> Ihrer Intuition richten wollen.

Ne faites pas attention aux indices si vous voulez
suivre votre intuition.

One is only given as much knowledge as one can
take. That is the purpose of the veil.

> Man erhält nur so viel Wissen, wie man ertragen
> kann. Das ist die Aufgabe des Schleiers.

Il nous est donné seulement autant de connaissance que nous sommes capables d'absorber ;c'est
le pourquoi du voile.

One cannot help a person who is suffering unless
one knows suffering and joy also.

> Man kann niemandem helfen, der leidet, wenn
> man nicht auch selbst Leid und Freude kennt.

On ne peut aider une personne qui souffre si l'on a
pas soi-même connu la peine et la joie.

Find accommodation for all those hearts that you
have touched upon; they have become part of your
being forever.

> Finden Sie Raum in sich für alle Herzen, mit de-
> nen Sie in Berührung gekommen sind: Sie sind für
> immer ein Teil von Ihnen geworden.

Trouvez un abri pour tous les cœurs que vous avez
touchés ; ils font désormais partie de votre être pour
toujours.

We might be the leading edge in bringing about
the purpose of the universe.

> Vielleicht sind wir in einer Vorreiterrolle dabei,
> den Sinn des Universums hervorzubringen.

Peut-être sommes-nous à l'avant-garde pour réaliser le dessein de l'univers.

We cannot free ourselves from our identification
with our individual self unless we open ourselves
to the infinite dimension of the power of the
sacred.

> Wir können uns nicht von der Identifikation mit
> unserem individuellen Selbst befreien, ohne uns
> der unendlichen Dimension der Macht der Heilig-
> keit zu öffnen.

Nous ne pouvons pas nous libérer de l'identification avec notre être individuel, si nous ne nous
ouvrons pas à la dimension infinie de la puissance
du sacré.

Essence

There is a condition for survival after death: the
truth body survives, so if it's not very strong, then
there's not much survival.

> Es gibt eine Vorbedingung für das Überleben
> nach dem Tod: es ist der Wahrheitskörper, der
> überlebt. Wenn dieser nicht sehr stark ist, gibt es
> deshalb auch nicht viel, das überlebt.

Il y a une condition à la survie après la mort :
puisque c'est le corps de vérité qui survit si celui-ci
n'est pas assez fort la survie sera faible.

I sometimes wonder if our quest for awakening is
not the highest egoism.

> Manchmal frage ich mich, ob unser Streben nach
> Erwachen nicht der größte Egoismus ist.

Je me demande parfois si notre quête d'éveil n'est
pas le plus haut degré de l'égoïsme.

Meditation takes us to the dimensions where the
irreconcilables reconcile.

> Meditation führt uns in Dimensionen, in denen
> das Unvereinbare vereinbar ist.

La méditation nous transporte sur une dimension
où les irréconciliables se réconcilient.

In the immaculate place of one's being there is an
innocent child who can't be wounded, sullied or
tarnished.

> An einem reinen Ort unseres Wesens gibt es ein
> unschuldiges Kind, das weder verletzt, befleckt
> noch beschmutzt werden kann.

Dans le lieu immaculé de notre être se trouve un
enfant innocent qui ne peut être ni blessé, ni souil-
lé, ni terni.

Awakening to the Sufis means the everywhere and always manifests in the here and now.

> Erwachen bedeutet für die Sufis, dass sich das „Überallige und Immerige" im „Hier und Jetzt" verwirklicht.

Pour les soufis, l'éveil signifie que le « partout et toujours » se manifeste dans le « ici et maintenant.»

The Instant of Time is a sharp sword that frees you, both from the conditioning of the past and the constraint that you have imposed upon yourself by your own planning.

> Der unmittelbare Augenblick ist ein scharfes Schwert, das Sie befreit, sowohl von der Prägung durch die Vergangenheit, als auch von den Beschränkungen, die Sie sich durch Ihr eigenes Planen selbst auferlegt haben.

L'Instant de Temps est une épée acérée qui vous libère du conditionnement du passé aussi bien que de la contrainte que vous vous êtes imposée en planifiant.

Though you may not change it, you can handle an
ugly situation beautifully.

> Auch wenn Sie vielleicht eine hässliche Situation
> nicht ändern können, so können Sie doch schön
> mit ihr umgehen.

Il se peut que vous ne puissiez pas transformer
une situation désagréable, mais vous pouvez la
manier avec délicatesse.

What a risk God takes in giving us freedom!

> Was geht Gott für ein Risiko ein, indem Er uns
> Freiheit gibt!

Quel risque Dieu prend-t-il en nous donnant la
liberté !

The ego is important until one does not need it
anymore.

> Das Ego ist solange wichtig, bis man es nicht mehr
> braucht.

L'ego est important seulement aussi longtemps
qu'on en a besoin.

We offer an obstacle to God's experiencing fulfillment if we do not fully experience our own
identity.

> Solange wir unsere eigene Identität nicht vollstän-
> dig durchleben, hindern wir Gott daran, Vollen-
> dung zu erfahren.

Nous représentons un obstacle à l'expérience divine de la réalisation, si nous ne faisons pas pleine-
ment l'expérience de notre identité.

How does one know if one's intuition rings true?
By one's scruple about truthfulness, one develops
a sense of authenticity.

> Woher weiß man, ob man mit seiner Intuition
> richtig liegt? Durch einen gewissenhaften Umgang
> mit Ehrlichkeit entwickelt man ein Gefühl für
> Echtheit.

Comment savons-nous si notre intuition sonne
juste ? C'est en ayant des scrupules quant à la vé-
racité (des choses) que nous développons l'authenticité.

If love for God seems beyond your grasp, then
know that it is there in every act of love.

> Wenn Ihnen die Liebe zu Gott unfassbar er-
> scheint, dann denken Sie daran, dass sie in jedem
> Ausdruck der Liebe enthalten ist.

Si l'amour pour Dieu vous semble hors de portée,
sachez qu'il se trouve dans chaque acte d'amour.

If your heart is burning in the ecstasy of love, it
will open the hearts of all beings.

> Wenn Ihr Herz in der Ekstase der Liebe brennt,
> öffnet es die Herzen aller Wesen.

Si votre cœur brûle dans l'extase de l'amour, il ou-
vrira le cœur de tous les êtres.

Perhaps the basic energy of the universe is not
light, but ecstasy; light is ecstasy.

> Vielleicht ist die grundlegende Energie des Uni-
> versums nicht Licht, sondern Ekstase. Licht ist
> Ekstase.

Peut-être que l'énergie de base de l'univers n'est
pas la lumière mais plutôt l'extase ; la lumière est
extase.

There are beings who do not exist on the physical plane but have their being on other planes; we have our being on all planes.

> Es gibt Wesen, die nicht auf der physischen Ebene existieren, sondern auf anderen Ebenen: Wir leben auf allen Ebenen.

Il y a des êtres qui n'existent pas sur le plan physique mais qui existent sur d'autres dimensions ; notre être s'étend sur toutes les dimensions.

There is a place in us that can never be tarnished.

> Es gibt einen Ort in uns, der niemals beschmutzt werden kann.

Il y a en nous un lieu qui ne peut jamais être terni.

Perhaps the ultimate relaxation is the relaxation of our sense of identity.

> Vielleicht ist die letztendliche Entspannung die Lockerung unseres Identitätsgefühls.

Peut-être que la relaxation ultime est la relaxation de notre sens de l'identité.

The world of imagination is the software of the universe.

      Die Welt der Imagination ist die Software des Universums.

Le monde de l'imagination est le logiciel de l'univers.

Awakening and creativity are the two poles of life's activity.

      Erwachen und Kreativität sind die beiden Pole der Lebensenergie.

L'éveil et la créativité sont les deux pôles de l'activité de la vie.

Sufis see the whole universe as the divine nostalgia for self-discovery.

      Sufis verstehen das ganze Universum als die göttliche Sehnsucht nach Selbstentdeckung.

Les soufis voient l'univers entier comme l'aspiration divine à la découverte de Soi.

Grace is very difficult to understand; it's an expression of freedom behind law.

> Gnade ist sehr schwer zu verstehen; sie ist ein Ausdruck von Freiheit hinter dem Gesetz.

La grâce est difficle à comprendre ; elle est une expression de la liberté au-delà de la loi.

If you think of God as the Creator, then you must also think of God as the Sustainer, because one is continually being recreated.

> Wenn Sie sich Gott als Schöpfer vorstellen, dann müssen Sie sich Gott auch als Erhalter vorstellen, denn wir werden ständig neu erschaffen.

Si vous pensez à Dieu comme au Créateur, vous devez aussi penser à Dieu comme à Celui qui maintient et soutient, car vous êtes continuellement recréés.

The heart experiences emotion at the sight of
beauty, whereas the soul experiences emotion
when it is faced with light.

> Das Herz wird von Schönheit berührt, während
> die Seele von der Begegnung mit Licht berührt
> wird.

Le cœur s'émeut à la vue de la beauté ; tandis que
l'âme s'émeut devant la lumière.

To make God a reality we try to express in a form
that which is beyond form.

> Um Gott zu einer Wirklichkeit zu machen, versu-
> chen wir das, was jenseits von Form ist, in Form
> auszudrücken.

Afin de faire de Dieu une réalité nous tentons
d'exprimer dans une forme ce qui est au-delà de
la forme.

As one evolves, one becomes more and more
spirit.

> Wenn man sich weiterentwickelt, wird man im-
> mer mehr zu einem geistigen Wesen.

En évoluant, on devient de plus en plus esprit.

The clue is shifting one's self-image, one's identity:
perceive yourself as the essence.

> Der Schlüssel liegt darin, das Selbstbild, die eigene
> Identität zu verlagern: Nehmen Sie sich selbst als
> die Essenz wahr.

La clef c'est de modifier l'image que l'on a de soi,
de changer sa propre identité : se percevoir comme
étant l'essence.

Peace helps one overcome the feeling of being
subjected to impressions from outside.

> Frieden hilft uns, das Gefühl zu überwinden, den
> Eindrücken von außen ausgeliefert zu sein.

La paix nous aide à surmonter le sentiment
d'être assujettis aux impressions qui viennent de
l'extérieur.

The human being is the exemplification of God.

> Der Mensch ist die Veranschaulichung Gottes.

L'être humain est à l'exemple de Dieu.

We are always concealing our feelings behind our
thoughts.

> Wir verbergen unsere Gefühle immer hinter un-
> seren Gedanken.

Nous cachons toujours nos sentiments derrière
nos pensées.

The emotion of vastness frees one from a sense of
inadequacy.

> Die Emotion unermesslicher Weite befreit uns
> von dem Gefühl der Unzulänglichkeit.

L'émotion devant l'immensité nous libère du sentiment d'être limités.

We would not be creative if our only purpose in
life is to be what we already are.

> Wir wären nicht schöpferisch, wenn unser einzi-
> ger Zweck im Leben wäre, das zu sein, was wir be-
> reits sind.

Nous ne serions pas créatifs si notre seul but dans
la vie était d'être ce que nous sommes déjà.

You are another me; I am another you.

Du bist ein anderes Ich; Ich bin ein anderes Du.

Vous êtres un autre moi ; je suis un autre vous.

It is only when one is in a high state that one's judgment is reliable.

Nur wenn man in einem hohen Zustand ist, ist das eigene Urteil verlässlich.

C'est seulement lorsque nous nous trouvons dans un état d'élévation que notre jugement est fiable.

When we want to change another person, we are showing a lack of respect for them and what is important to them in their past, present and future.

Wenn wir eine andere Person ändern wollen, zeigen wir einen Mangel an Respekt vor ihr und was für sie in ihrer Vergangenheit, Gegenwart und Zukunft wichtig ist.

Lorsque nous voulons changer une personne, nous faisons preuve d'un manque de respect pour elle, et pour ce qui, dans son passé, son présent et son futur, est important pour elle.

Cherish others, uphold them, guard them against humiliation.

Schätzen Sie andere wert, halten Sie sie in Ehren, schützen Sie sie vor Demütigung.

Chérissez les autres, prenez soin d'eux, protégez-les contre l'humiliation.

Mastery consists in never giving in to self-pity.

Meisterschaft besteht darin, sich niemals dem Selbstmitleid zu überlassen.

La maîtrise consiste à ne jamais se laisser aller à s'apitoyer sur soi-même.

Let your peace be materialized in actions.

Lassen Sie Ihren Frieden zu Handlungen werden.

Faites que votre paix se matérialise en actions.

Instead of lamenting your fate, create your world.

> Erschaffen Sie Ihre Welt, anstatt sich über Ihr Schicksal zu beklagen.

Plutôt que de vous lamenter sur votre destinée, créez le monde (auquel vous aspirez).

Creativity is always taking a risk.

> Kreativität geht immer ein Risiko ein.

La créativité prend toujours un risque.

Of all the qualities in your being, the one that is most God-like is creativity.

> Von allen Qualitäten Ihres Wesens ist die Schöpferkraft diejenige, die am gottähnlichsten ist.

Parmi toutes les qualités de votre être, celle qui s'apparente le plus à Dieu est la créativité.

We need a new way of communication, which is
not experience but communion.

> Wir brauchen eine neue Art der Kommunikation,
> die keine Erfahrung sondern Kommunion ist.

Nous avons besoin d'une nouvelle sorte de communication qui ne soit pas une expérience mais
une communion.

We are the light of the stars.

> Wir sind das Licht der Sterne.

Nous sommes la lumière des étoiles.

Your power is limited by your objective. If your
objective is service, the power that comes through
you is unlimited.

> Ihre Kraft wird durch Ihre Zielvorstellung be-
> grenzt. Wenn Dienen Ihr Ziel ist, ist die Kraft, die
> durch Sie durchkommt, unbegrenzt.

Votre puissance est limitée par votre objectif. Si
votre objectif est de servir, la puissance qui émane
de vous est illimitée.

The angels acquire wisdom by incarnating.

Engel erwerben Weisheit, indem sie inkarnieren.

Les anges acquièrent la sagesse en s'incarnant.

Just imagine yourself as the fulfillment of the
Divine Purpose.

Stellen Sie sich vor, Sie sind die Verwirklichung
der göttlichen Absicht!

Imaginez-vous comme étant la réalisation de
l'intention divine.

Discover God instead of believing in God.

Entdecken Sie Gott anstatt an Gott zu glauben.

Découvrez Dieu au lieu de croire en Dieu.

We must not confuse our concept of God with
God; use it as a stepping-stone, and then let it go.

> Wir dürfen unsere Vorstellung von Gott nicht mit
> Gott selbst verwechseln; nutzen Sie sie als Sprung-
> brett und lassen Sie sie dann los.

Il ne faut pas confondre le concept de Dieu avec
Dieu ; utilisez le comme un tremplin que vous
abandonnerez ensuite.

When creativity is done with excellence, splendor
breaks through.

> Wenn Kreativität vortrefflich ausgeführt wird,
> bricht Herrlichkeit hindurch.

Lorsque la créativité se manifeste de manière ex-
cellente, la splendeur se fait jour.

Ecstasy carries you to higher spheres where you
leave your will behind.

> Ekstase erhebt Sie in höhere Sphären, wo Sie Ihren
> Willen zurücklassen.

L'extase vous élève vers les hautes sphères ; là, vous
laissez votre volonté derrière vous.

Every atom, planet, galaxy is yearning for awakening; not only you, but the whole universe yearns to awaken.

> Jedes Atom, jeder Planet, jede Galaxie sehnt sich nach Erwachen; nicht nur Sie, sondern das ganze Universum sehnt sich danach, zu erwachen.

Chaque atome, chaque planète et chaque galaxie aspire à l'éveil ; pas seulement vous, mais tout l'univers aspire à s'éveiller.

Transformation is brought about by being in the presence of God.

> Transformation geschieht durch das Verweilen in der Gegenwart Gottes.

La transformation a lieu lorsque l'on vit dans la présence de Dieu.

All creativity is the result of imagination.

> Alle Kreativität ist das Ergebnis von Vorstellungskraft.

Toute créativité est le résultat de l'imagination.

You become what you concentrate on. Concentrate on God and you become God.

> Sie werden zu dem, worauf Sie sich konzentrieren. Konzentrieren Sie sich auf Gott, und Sie werden Gott.

Vous devenez ce sur quoi vous vous concentrez. Concentrez-vous sur Dieu et vous deviendrez Dieu.

The power of your light lies beyond the control of your will.

> Die Kraft Ihres Lichtes liegt außerhalb der Kontrolle Ihres Willens.

La puissance de votre lumière se trouve au-delà du contrôle de votre volonté.

Divine Will and human will are two dimensions of the same thing.

> Göttlicher Wille und menschlicher Wille sind zwei Dimensionen derselben Sache.

La volonté divine et la volonté humaine sont deux dimensions d'une même chose.

Music is the language of the soul and therefore it
communicates to us something that could never
be communicated in words.

> Musik ist die Sprache der Seele, und daher ver-
> mittelt sie uns etwas, das niemals mit Worten ver-
> mittelt werden könnte.

La musique est le langage de l'âme, c'est pour cela
qu'elle nous communique quelque chose qui ne
pourrait jamais être communiqué par les mots.

The symphony of the spheres is made of all the
cries of glee upon discovery.

> Die Symphonie der Sphären besteht aus all den
> Freudenrufen über gemachte Entdeckungen.

La symphonie des sphères est faite de tous les cris
de joie lors d'une découverte.

The ultimate mantram is the sound of the cry of
glory.

> Der Klang des Ausrufs der Verherrlichung ist das
> ultimative Mantra.

Le mantra ultime est le son du cri de gloire.

Have your strength in your heart, not in your head.

      Ihre Stärke sei in Ihrem Herzen, nicht in Ihrem Kopf.

Que votre force soit dans votre cœur et non pas dans votre tête.

Pain makes the soul sincere.

      Schmerz macht die Seele wahrhaftig.

La peine rend l'âme sincere.

Shake your soul! Awaken it from slumber! The time has come to awaken to your divine being.

      Rütteln Sie Ihre Seele auf! Erwecken Sie sie aus dem Schlaf! Es ist an der Zeit, zu Ihrem göttlichen Wesen zu erwachen.

Secouez votre âme ! Réveillez-la du sommeil ! Le temps est venu de vous éveiller à votre être divin.

The divine in us is what we can rely on.

Das, worauf wir uns verlassen können, ist das Göttliche in uns.

Le divin en nous, c'est à cela que nous pouvons nous fier.

In some challenging situations you can be very kind and gentle by not giving in.

In manchen schwierigen Situationen kann es sehr freundlich und schonend sein, nicht nachzugeben.

Dans certaines situations difficiles, vous serez aimables et bons en ne cédant pas.

You can't know the defects of a person without having them yourself.

Man kann um die Fehler eines Anderen nicht wissen, ohne sie selbst zu haben.

Vous ne pouvez pas connaître les défauts d'une personne si vous ne les avez pas vous-mêmes.

Can you imagine a being whose light is more radiant than, suns? That's an archangel. You carry the inheritance of that being.

> Können Sie sich ein Wesen vorstellen, dessen Licht heller strahlt als das vieler Sonnen? Das ist ein Erzengel. Sie tragen die Erbschaft dieses Wesens in sich.

Pouvez-vous imaginer un être dont la lumière rayonnerait plus que plusieurs soleils réunis ? Tel est l'archange. Vous portez en vous l'héritage de cet être.

The ultimate meditation is "Who am I?"

> Die ultimative Meditation ist „Wer bin ich?"

La méditation ultime est : « Qui suis-je ? »

The thought of dissolving, not holding on, overcomes greed.

> Der Gedanke daran loszulassen, anstatt festzuhalten, überwindet Habsucht.

La pensée de lâcher prise, plutôt que de tenir ferme, vient à bout de l'avidité.

Service is the opposite of greed.

Dienen ist das Gegenteil von Habsucht.

Le service est le contraire de l'avidité.

The problem is not the situation, but how one handles the situation.

Nicht die Situation ist das Problem, sondern wie man mit der Situation umgeht.

Le problème n'est pas la situation mais la façon dont on fait face à cette situation.

You have to find enough freedom in yourself to be able to free others.

Man muss genügend Freiheit in sich selbst finden, um andere befreien zu können.

Vous devez trouver en vous assez de liberté pour être capables de libérer autrui.

The whole of life is a process whereby the unman-
ifest becomes manifest.

> Das ganze Leben ist ein Vorgang, durch den das
> Nicht Offenbare offenbar wird.

Toute la vie est un processus à travers lequel ce qui
est non manifesté devient manifesté.

When one loves, one abstains from judging. The
"knowledge" that you have of a person, without
love for that person, is judgment.

> Wer liebt, urteilt nicht. Die "Kenntnis", die man
> von einem Menschen hat, ohne ihn zu lieben, ist
> ein Urteil.

Lorsque l'on aime, on ne juge pas. Sans amour la «
connaissance » que vous avez d'une personne est
jugement.

A closed heart means not trusting oneself to love.

> Ein verschlossenes Herz bedeutet, dass man sich
> der Liebe nicht anvertraut.

Avoir un cœur fermé signifie que l'on ne se sent
pas capable d'aimer.

When the sun is not in the sky, then one can see
the stars.

> Wenn die Sonne nicht am Himmel steht, kann
> man die Sterne sehen.

Quand le soleil n'est pas dans le ciel, on peut voir
les étoiles.

The magnificence of the Universe is in you.

> Die Herrlichkeit des Universums ist in Ihnen.

La magnificence de l'univers est en vous.

Science deals with predictables; creativity deals
with unpredictables.

> Wissenschaft befasst sich mit Vorhersagbarem,
> Kreativität mit Unvorhersagbarem.

La science s'occupe de ce qui est prévisible ; la
créativité s'occupe de ce qui est imprévisible.

The only way to hear the voice of glory is to sing it
ourselves.

Die einzige Möglichkeit, die Stimme der Herrlichkeit zu hören, ist sie selbst zu singen.

La seule façon d'entendre la voix de la gloire c'est
de chanter cette gloire nous-mêmes.

Freedom gives infinite power; it can move
mountains.

Freiheit verleiht unendliche Macht; sie kann Berge
versetzen.

La liberté confère une puissance infinie ; elle peut
déplacer les montagnes.

Healing is a combination of joy and peace. Joy in our relationship with the outside and peace in our discovery of the springhead of our being.

> Heilung ist eine Verbindung von Freude und Frieden. Freude in der Beziehung zur Außenwelt und Frieden im Entdecken des Ursprungs unseres Wesens.

La guérison est un alliage de joie et de paix ; joie dans la relation que nous entretenons avec le monde extérieur et paix lorsque nous découvrons la source de notre être.

Your domain is as wide as the influence of your soul; the higher the soul is attuned, the greater the domain.

> Ihr Zuständigkeitsbereich ist so weit wie der Einfluss Ihrer Seele: Je höher die Seele eingestimmt ist, desto größer ist dieser Bereich.

Votre domaine est aussi grand que l'est l'influence de votre âme ; plus votre âme est accordée sur un plan élevé, plus grand est votre domaine.

Our soul can be robbed of its power by resentment.

Unsere Seele kann durch Ärger ihrer Kraft beraubt werden.

Le ressentiment peut dérober à l'âme sa puissance.

Your intuition is the revelation of your own spirit.

Ihre Intuition ist die Offenbarung Ihres eigenen Geistes.

Votre intuition est la révélation de votre propre esprit.

The purpose of imagination is to transform the uncreated into a form.

Der Zweck der Vorstellungskraft ist es, dem Unerschaffenen eine Form zu geben.

Le but de l'imagination est de donner une forme à l'incréé.

The light of awareness, the light of consciousness
arises out of a broken heart; the heart, by breaking,
becomes an ocean, accommodating all beings.

> Das Licht des Gewahrseins, das Licht des Be-
> wusstseins steigt aus einem gebrochenen Herzen
> auf; indem das Herz bricht, wird es zu einem Oze-
> an, der alle Wesen in sich aufnimmt.

La lumière de l'éveil, la lumière de la conscience,
s'élève d'un cœur brisé ; le cœur, en se brisant, devient un océan qui accueille tous les êtres.

Light arises in your soul as a consequence of the
striking of the heart.

> Wenn das Herz getroffen wird, steigt Licht in Ih-
> rer Seele auf.

La lumière s'élève dans votre âme lorsque votre
cœur a été touché.

The universe is breathing in you on several planes
at the same time.

> Das Universum atmet in Ihnen auf mehreren Ebe-
> nen gleichzeitig.

L'univers respire en vous, sur plusieurs niveaux en
même temps.

Christ dances on the cross - He doesn't hang there
- times have changed.

> Christus tanzt am Kreuz – Er hängt nicht dort –
> die Zeiten haben sich geändert.

Le Christ danse sur la croix – Il n'y est pas cloué –
les temps ont changé.

Your circumstances are a reflection of what you
are in yourself.

> Ihre Umstände sind ein Spiegel dessen, was Sie in
> Ihrem Inneren sind.

Les circonstances de votre vie sont le reflet de ce
que vous êtes profondément vous-mêmes.

Spiritual progress comes by changing one's point
of view.

> Spiritueller Fortschritt stellt sich ein, wenn man
> den Standpunkt wechselt.

Le progrès spirituel a lieu lorsque l'on change son
point de vue.

We are the transducer between universal light and universal matter.

> Wir sind die Umwandler zwischen universellem Licht und universeller Materie.

Nous sommes les transducteurs entre la lumière universelle et la matière universelle.

Hear the sound of the universe in your heart.

> Hören Sie den Klang des Universums in Ihrem Herzen.

Ecoutez le son de l'univers dans votre cœur.

There is no door that the heart cannot open when it has become so living that it is the Divine Ocean.

> Es gibt keine Tür, die das Herz nicht öffnen kann, wenn es so lebendig geworden ist, dass es zum göttlichen Ozean wurde.

Il n'y a pas de porte qui ne puisse être ouverte par le cœur, lorsque celui-ci est devenu tellement vivant qu'il est semblable à l'Océan Divin.

The first principle in healing is joy.

Die wichtigste Grundlage für Heilung ist Freude.

Le premier principe de guérison est la joie.

We don't love the tree because of its beauty, but
for the being of the tree.

Wir lieben den Baum nicht wegen seiner Schönheit, sondern wegen seines Wesens als Baum.

Nous n'aimons par l'arbre pour sa beauté mais
pour son être en tant qu'arbre.

Get into a state of passive volition, which means
unintentionally pursuing one's intention.

Versetzen Sie sich in einen Zustand passiven Wol-
lens. Das bedeutet, absichtslos seine Absicht zu
verfolgen.

Mettez-vous en état de volition passive, ce qui signifie que poursuivez vos intentions de manière
non intentionnelle.

Find your relationship with the universe, which
has nothing to do with space at all.

> Entdecken Sie Ihre Beziehung zu dem Universum,
> das überhaupt nichts mit Raum zu tun hat.

Découvrez votre relation avec l'univers, qui n'a
rien à voir avec l'espace.

Let yourself grasp immensity, the immensity of
which you are an expression.

> Erlauben Sie sich, Unermesslichkeit zu erfassen,
> jene Unermesslichkeit, von der Sie selbst ein Aus-
> druck sind.

Saisissez l'immensité, l'immensité dont vous êtes
l'expression.

The rishi can observe a flower opening under his
glance. That can be your experience.

> Der Rishi kann beobachten, wie sich unter seinem
> Blick eine Blume öffnet. Diese Erfahrung können
> auch Sie machen.

Le Rishi peut observer une fleur s'ouvrir sous son
regard. Vous pouvez aussi faire cette expérience.

We are the convergence of the whole universe. We all have a great need for immensity.

> In uns läuft das gesamte Universum zusammen. Wir alle haben ein großes Bedürfnis nach Unermesslichkeit.

Nous sommes la convergence de tout l'univers. Nous avons tous un grand besoin d'immensité.

Perhaps it is written in our programming: to transmute personal love into divine emotion.

> Vielleicht ist es in unsere Programmierung eingeschrieben, persönliche Liebe in göttliche Emotion zu verwandeln.

Peut-être qu'il est écrit dans notre programmation qu'il s'agit de transmuter l'amour personnel en émotion divine.

The atoms themselves are endowed with intelligence, consciousness, and even emotion.

Selbst die Atome sind mit Intelligenz, Bewusstsein und sogar Emotion ausgestattet.

Les atomes eux aussi sont dotés d'intelligence, de conscience et même d'émotion.

If you cannot love all beings, you can express divine love in forgiveness, which means to purify your heart of grudges against any being.

Wenn Sie nicht alle Wesen lieben können, dann können Sie göttliche Liebe durch Vergebung zum Ausdruck bringen. Das bedeutet, das Herz von Groll gegenüber allen Lebewesen zu reinigen.

Si vous ne pouvez pas aimer tous les êtres, vous pouvez exprimer l'amour divin dans le pardon ; ce qui signifie que vous devez purifier votre cœur de la rancune envers qui que ce soit.

Truth will make you free, but it will also make you suffer.

Wahrheit wird Sie befreien, aber sie wird Sie auch leiden lassen.

La vérité vous rendra libre, mais elle vous fera aussi souffrir.

Music teaches us that conflicts are part of harmony.

> Musik lehrt uns, dass Konflikte Teil der Harmonie sind.

La musique nous enseigne que les conflits font partie de l'harmonie.

One can get into the emotion that has become a flower; that is the experience of the mystic and the dervish.

> Man kann in die Emotion eintauchen, die zu einer Blume wurde; das ist das Erleben des Mystikers und des Derwisch.

On peut entrer dans l'émotion qui est devenue fleur ; c'est là l'expérience que fait le mystique et le derviche.

Even our bodies are endowed with the rhythms of the symphony of the spheres, the language of God.

> Sogar unser Körper ist erfüllt von den Rhythmen der Symphonie der Sphären, der Sprache Gottes.

Même notre corps est doté des rythmes de la symphonie des sphères, le langage de Dieu.

We can discover in ourselves what we perceive in
the cosmos.

> All das, was wir im Kosmos wahrnehmen, können
> wir auch in uns selbst entdecken.

Nous pouvons découvrir en nous ce que nous per-
cevons dans le cosmos.

We can reach any being, any person, from inside
ourselves.

> Wir können jedes Wesen, jede Person von unse-
> rem Inneren her erreichen.

Nous pouvons atteindre tout être, toute personne
à partir des profondeurs de notre être.

Truthfulness develops intuition.

> Wahrhaftigkeit entwickelt die Intuition.

L'authenticité développe l'intuition.

Have the courage to face the light of your own being.

Haben Sie den Mut, dem Licht Ihres eigenen Wesens zu begegnen.

Ayez le courage de faire face à la lumière de votre être.

It is wise to balance mastery with intuition.

Es ist weise, Meisterschaft mit Intuition auszugleichen.

Il est sage d'équilibrer la maîtrise avec l'intuition.

The best use of intuition is as a warning.

Der beste Nutzen von Intuition ist die Warnung.

L'intuition est utilisée au mieux dans l'avertissement.

One cannot reach one's highest self without having found peace in oneself.

> Man kann sein höchstes Selbst nicht erreichen,
> ohne inneren Frieden gefunden zu haben.

On ne peut atteindre son être le plus haut sans
avoir trouvé la paix en soi.

The beauty that comes through the mind inspired
by ecstasy is monumental.

> Die Schönheit, die durch einen von Ekstase inspi-
> rierten Geist vermittelt wird, ist gewaltig.

La beauté qui vient d'un esprit inspiré par l'extase
est merveilleuse.

Creativity is the thrust of ecstasy and making it an
actuality in our lives.

> Kreativität ist die Schubkraft der Ekstase und
> macht diese zu einer Wirklichkeit in unserem
> Leben.

La créativité c'est la montée de l'extase, et c'est le
fait de l'actualiser dans notre vie.

Ecstasy is triggered off every time one rises above
oneself.

Jedes Mal, wenn man sich über sich selbst erhebt,
wird Ekstase ausgelöst.

L'extase est déclenchée à chaque fois que nous
nous élevons au-dessus de nous-mêmes.

We can realize ourselves as extensions of the universe as God.

Wir können uns selbst als Erweiterung des Universums als Gott verstehen.

Nous pouvons nous réaliser comme des extensions de l'univers qui est Dieu.

God's presence is all-pervading, whether there is
manifestation or not; it is very mysterious.

Gottes Gegenwart ist alldurchdringend, unabhän-
gig von Manifestation oder nicht. Es ist ein großes
Mysterium.

La présence de Dieu est toute pénétrante, qu'il y
ait manifestation ou non ; ceci est très mystérieux.

Think of yourself as a soul instead of a person.

       Denken Sie sich selbst als Seele anstatt als Person.

Pensez à vous comme à une âme plutôt que comme à une personne.

The purpose of life is that God should attain through you a further advance in the evolution of the universe.

       Der Zweck des Lebens ist, dass Gott durch uns einen weiteren Fortschritt in der Evolution des Universums machen kann.

Le but de la vie est que Dieu atteigne un plus grand avancement dans l'évolution de l'univers, grâce à vous.

Quintessence

Let your power come through as the manifestation of truth.

> Lassen Sie Ihre Kraft als Manifestation der Wirk-
> lichkeit durchbrechen.

Révélez votre puissance comme manifestation de
la vérité.

Experience yourself as the divine intention.

> Erfahren Sie sich selbst als göttliche Absicht.

Faites l'expérience de vous-mêmes comme intention divine.

Experience the condition of the universe inside
yourself.

> Erfahren Sie den Zustand des Universums in Ih-
> rem Inneren.

Faites l'expérience de la condition de l'univers en
vous-mêmes.

The only evil is harming another or yourself, another soul or your own soul.

> Das einzige Übel ist, jemand anderen oder sich selbst zu verletzen, eine andere oder die eigene Seele.

Le seul mal est de nuire à autrui, ou à vous-mêmes ; à une autre âme ou à la vôtre.

Always be conscious of your eternal being.

> Seien Sie sich immer Ihres ewigen Wesens bewusst.

Soyez toujours conscients de votre être éternel.

Divine Creativity is completed by human creativity.

> Göttliche Schöpferkraft wird durch menschliche Schöpferkraft vervollständigt.

La créativité divine est complétée par la créativité humaine.

We are a dome in which the music of the spheres resounds.

> Wir sind ein Dom, in dem die Musik der Sphären widerhallt.

Nous sommes un dôme dans lequel résonne la musique des sphères.

The whole purpose of life is for God to emerge as us.

> Der ganze Sinn des Lebens besteht darin, dass Gott als uns in Erscheinung tritt.

Tout le but de la vie est que Dieu émerge en et par nous.

We discover beauty as we create it.

> Wir entdecken Schönheit, indem wir sie erschaffen.

Nous découvrons la beauté en la créant.

Ecstasy is total involvement, taking the plunge, re-
lentlessly coping with the odds, dauntlessly riding
the tide of adversity.

> Ekstase ist vollständiges Sich-Einlassen, den
> Sprung zu wagen, sich schonungslos allen Schwie-
> rigkeiten zu stellen, furchtlos die Welle der Wid-
> rigkeiten zu reiten.

L'extase c'est l'engagement total : c'est plonger en
faisant courageusement face à tout ce qui peut sur-
gir ; c'est chevaucher les vagues de l'adversité.

Communicate beauty by being in love with beauty, which means being in love with God; that is the
ultimate Beauty.

> Vermitteln Sie Schönheit, indem Sie in Schönheit
> verliebt sind. Dies bedeutet, dass Sie in Gott ver-
> liebt sind; das ist ultimative Schönheit.

Communiquez la beauté en étant amoureux de la
beauté, ce qui signifie aussi, en étant amoureux de
Dieu ; ceci est la beauté ultime.

There's no outside, there is no inside: once the heart has become the ocean of life, it accommodates all things and all beings.

> Es gibt kein Außen und kein Innen: Wenn das Herz einmal zum Ozean des Lebens geworden ist, beherbergt es alle Dinge und alle Wesen.

Il n'y a pas d'extérieur, il n'y a pas d'intérieur : devenu l'océan de vie, le cœur accueille toutes les choses et tous les êtres.

The whole universe was created for the purpose of illumination.

> Das ganze Universum wurde für den Zweck der Erleuchtung erschaffen.

L'univers entier a été créé en vue de l'illumination.

Life attains its summit in magnanimity.

> Das Leben erreicht seinen Höhepunkt in Großmut.

La vie atteint son apogée dans la magnanimité.

To be a lover one needs to be a master.

> Um ein Liebender zu sein, muss man ein Meister sein.

Pour être un amoureux, il faut être un maître.

Think of peace as power.

> Denken Sie an Frieden als eine Macht.

Pensez à la paix comme à une puissance.

There are no objects, only beings!

> Es gibt keine Dinge, nur Wesen!

Il n'y a pas d'objets, il n'y a que des êtres !

To gain insight, the mystic goes to the depths of the universe.

> Um Einsicht zu gewinnen, taucht der Mystiker in die Tiefen des Universums.

Pour atteindre la vue intérieure, le mystique plonge dans les profondeurs de l'univers.

We are not here for ourselves.

> Wir sind nicht um unserer selbst willen hier.

Nous ne sommes pas ici pour nous-mêmes.

You are the artist, you are the raw material, you
are the work of art and you are the reality behind
the work of art.

> Sie sind der Künstler, Sie sind das Rohmaterial,
> Sie sind das Kunstwerk und Sie sind die Wirklich-
> keit hinter dem Kunstwerk.

Vous êtes l'artiste, vous êtes le matériau brut, vous
êtes l'œuvre d'art et vous êtes la réalité derrière
l'œuvre d'art.

Never think of yourself as an individual different
from God.

> Denken Sie niemals von sich als ein Individuum,
> das von Gott verschieden ist.

Ne pensez jamais à vous comme à un individu dif-
férent de Dieu.

Face God and allow the divine action of God to
happen in you.

> Begegnen Sie Gott, und erlauben Sie Gott, in Ih-
> nen zu wirken.

Tournez-vous vers Dieu et laisser Dieu agir en
vous.

The more conscious we are of radiating light, the
more light we radiate.

> Je bewusster wir uns sind, dass wir Licht ausstrah-
> len, desto mehr Licht strahlen wir aus.

Plus nous sommes conscients d'émettre de la lumière, plus nous rayonnons de la lumière.

It is our ecstasy in the act of glorification that gives
us access to the level of pure splendor.

> Unsere Ekstase im Akt der Verherrlichung ist das,
> was uns Zugang zur Ebene reiner Herrlichkeit ge-
> währt.

C'est notre extase dans l'acte de glorification qui
nous donne accès à la dimension de pure splendeur.

The archangel of your being is your own soul.

Der Erzengel Ihres Wesens ist ihre eigene Seele.

L'archange de votre être est votre propre âme.

Love is the wine of the divine intoxication.

Liebe ist der Wein der göttlichen Trunkenheit.

L'amour est le vin de l'ivresse divine.

Your heart is no longer just your heart since it has
become the heart of the divine Beloved.

Ihr Herz ist nicht länger nur Ihr Herz, seit es zum
Herzen des göttlichen Geliebten geworden ist.

Votre cœur n'est plus seulement votre cœur, depuis qu'il est devenu le cœur du Bien-aimé.

See your problems in the light of what is happening in the whole universe.

> Betrachten Sie Ihre Probleme im Lichte dessen, was im gesamten Universum geschieht.

Voyez vos problèmes à la lumière de ce qui se passe dans tout l'univers.

Divine love is the effulgence behind all creation, behind all phenomena, and the light in the heart of those you love, whose light you enhance by your love.

> Göttliche Liebe ist der Glanz hinter aller Schöpfung, hinter allen Erscheinungen, und das Licht in den Herzen derer, die Sie lieben, deren Licht Sie durch Ihre Liebe verstärken.

L'amour divin est le rayonnement derrière toute la création, derrière tous les phénomènes ; cet amour divin est aussi la lumière dans le cœur de ceux que vous aimez, lumière que vous rendez plus brillante par votre amour.

Your own heart is the key to the hearts of all.

> Ihr eigenes Herz ist der Schlüssel zu den Herzen aller.

Votre cœur est la clé du cœur de tous.

The universe is breathing as you.

> Das Universum atmet als Sie.

Vous êtes l'univers qui respire.

When you are in a state of ecstasy your thoughts
are creative: then one's emotions and movements
reveal a cosmic harmony.

> Wenn Sie im Zustand der Ekstase sind, sind Ihre
> Gedanken schöpferisch: dann offenbaren Ihre
> Emotionen und Regungen kosmische Harmonie.

Lorsque vous êtes en état d'extase vos pensées sont
créatrices ; alors, vos émotions ainsi que vos mou-
vements révèlent une harmonie cosmique.

We not only transmit the thinking of the universe;
we contribute to that thinking in a personal way.

> Wir geben das Denken des Universums nicht nur
> weiter; wir tragen zu diesem Denken auch persön-
> lich bei.

Nous ne transmettons pas seulement la pensée de
l'univers ; nous contribuons de manière personnelle à cette pensée.

God is continually performing new acts of freedom, freeing people from the rigidity of Law. That
is grace.

> Gott befreit uns ständig aufs Neue, indem Er den
> Menschen von der Härte des Gesetzes befreit. Das
> ist Gnade.

Dieu accomplit continuellement de nouveaux
actes de liberté en libérant les êtres de la rigidité de
la Loi ; ceci est la grâce.

Grace means the opposite of Law.

> Gnade bedeutet das Gegenteil von Gesetz.

La grâce signifie le contraire de la loi.

God seeks fulfillment in the human being.

Gott sucht Erfüllung im Menschen.

Dieu cherche l'accomplissement en les êtres humains.

The emotion of glorification comes when we let the divine action take over. We prepare by purification, by lending ourselves to the divine operation.

Wenn wir erlauben, dass das Göttliche das Geschehen übernimmt, stellt sich die Emotion der Verherrlichung ein. Wir bereiten uns darauf durch Reinigung vor, indem wir uns selbst dem göttlichen Wirken überlassen.

L'émotion de glorification apparaît lorsque nous laissons l'action divine prendre l'ascendant en nous. Nous nous y préparons en nous purifiant et en nous prêtant à l'opération divine.

The discovery of the more transcendental dimensions of one's being is gained by doing: dedicating
oneself to service and acting on it.

> Die transzendenteren Dimensionen des eigenen
> Wesens werden im Tun erreicht: indem man sich
> dem Dienen weiht und entsprechend handelt.

La découverte des dimensions transcendantales
de notre être se fait dans l'action : en nous consa-
crant au service et en agissant en conséquence.

Be kind to your soul; your soul's need is
exaltation.

> Behandeln Sie Ihre Seele freundlich; Ihre Seele
> braucht Erhebung.

Soyez bon envers votre âme ; votre âme aspire à
l'exaltation.

Not just the eyes but the heart itself casts light
upon all things.

> Nicht nur die Augen – das Herz selbst wirft Licht
> auf alle Dinge.

Le cœur lui-même projette la lumière sur toutes
les choses, ce ne sont pas seulement les yeux qui
le font.

That which clarifies the soul is truthfulness.

Wahrhaftigkeit ist das, was die Seele klärt.

C'est la sincérité qui éclaircit l'âme.

We betray ourselves when we yearn to find a beloved outside.

Wir betrügen uns selbst, wenn wir uns danach sehnen, einen Geliebten im Äußeren zu finden.

Nous nous trahissons lorsque nous aspirons à trouver un bien-aimé en dehors de nous-mêmes.

God cannot be good and perfect at the same time.

Gott kann nicht gleichzeitig gütig und vollkommen sein.

Dieu ne peut pas être bon et parfait en même temps.

You experience yourself as matter experiencing
spirit and you experience yourself as spirit experiencing matter.

> Wir erfahren uns selbst als Materie, die Geist er-
> lebt, und wir erfahren uns als geistiges Wesen, das
> Materie erlebt.

Vous faites l'expérience de vous-mêmes en tant
que matière faisant l'expérience de l'esprit et vous
faites l'expérience de vous-mêmes en tant qu'esprit
faisant l'expérience de la matière.

One experiences ecstasy when one discovers the
creator in one, as oneself.

> Man erfährt Ekstase, wenn man den Schöpfer in
> sich selbst entdeckt - als sich selbst.

On fait l'expérience de l'extase lorsque que l'on découvre le créateur en soi, comme étant soi.

Ecstasy is the magic, out of which life is born,
the word that opens doors into unpredictable
perspectives.

> Ekstase ist die Magie, aus der das Leben geboren
> wird, das Wort, das Tore zu unvorhersehbaren
> Perspektiven öffnet.

L'extase est la magie qui donne la vie, elle est le
mot qui ouvre les portes sur des perspectives im-
prévisibles.

We are the image of God and God is our image.

> Wir sind das Ebenbild Gottes, und Gott ist unser
> Ebenbild.

Nous sommes à l'image de Dieu; et Dieu est à
notre image.

We get caught up in the light that is seen; we are
also the light that sees.

> Wir lassen uns vom sichtbaren Licht gefangen
> nehmen; wir sind aber auch das Licht, das sieht.

Nous nous laissons piéger par la lumière qui se
voit ; mais nous sommes aussi la lumière qui voit.

The key to the plane of splendor is not understanding, but ecstasy.

Der Schlüssel zur Ebene der Herrlichkeit ist nicht
Verständnis, sondern Ekstase.

La clef de la dimension de splendeur n'est pas la
compréhension, mais l'extase.

God finds completion in the human being.

Gott findet im menschlichen Wesen Vollendung.

Dieu trouve sa pleine réalisation dans l'être
humain.

The whole past of the universe is present in your
being.

Die gesamte Vergangenheit des Universums ist in
Ihrem Wesen gegenwärtig.

Tout le passé de l'univers est présent dans votre
être.

When we enter into the mind of God, we can act
in a way that enhances the divine intention.

> Wenn wir in die Denkweise Gottes gelangen, kön-
> nen wir auf eine Art handeln, die das göttliche
> Vorhaben bereichert.

Lorsque nous pénétrons dans l'esprit de Dieu,
nous pouvons agir de façon à rehausser l'intention
divine.

Ultimately, the only thing that makes sense in life
is glorification.

> Letzten Endes ist Verherrlichung das einzige, was
> im Leben Sinn macht.

Finalement, la seule chose qui donne un sens à la
vie c'est la glorification.

We come to identify with our planetary, solar, galactic, and even angelic inheritance as the boundaries of consciousness dissolve.

> In dem Maße, wie sich die Grenzen des Bewusstseins auflösen, identifizieren wir uns zunehmend mit unserer planetaren, solaren, galaktischen und sogar engelhaften Erbschaft.

Tandis que les frontières de la conscience se dissolvent, nous en venons à nous identifier à notre héritage planétaire, solaire, galactique, voire même angélique.

Out of love for your potentialities, God descended from the solitude of unknowing.

> Gott stieg aus Liebe zu Ihren Potentialen aus der Einsamkeit des Nichtwissens herab.

Par amour pour vos potentialités, Dieu est descendu de la solitude de l'inconnaissance.

Everything is linked with everything else, inextricably.

> Alles ist untrennbar mit allem verbunden.

Tout est est lié au tout, inextricablement.

There's no threshold between us and the universe.

Zwischen uns und dem Universum gibt es keine Schwelle.

Il n'y a pas de seuil entre nous et l'univers.

Rebirth takes place in the act of surrender.

Neugeburt geschieht im Akt der Hingabe.

La renaissance a lieu dans le don de soi.

God discovers His perfection in human imperfection.

Gott entdeckt Seine Vollkommenheit in menschlicher Unvollkommenheit.

Dieu découvre sa perfection dans l'imperfection humaine.

God cannot be limited by manifestation.

Gott kann durch Manifestation nicht begrenzt werden.

Dieu ne peut pas être limité par la manifestation.

About the Author

Pir Vilayat Inayat Khan (1916–2004) was the eldest son and spiritual successor of Hazrat Pir-O-Murshid Inayat Khan, the first Sufi master to teach in the West. Vilayat Inayat Khan was born in England and raised in France. He was educated at the Sorbonne, Oxford, and École Normale de Musique de Paris. During World War II he served in the British Royal Navy and was assigned the duties of mine sweeping during the invasion at Normandy. His sister, Noor Inayat Khan served in the French section of Britain's SOE (Special Operations Executive) as a radio operator. She was captured and executed in 1944 at Dachau concentration camp.

After the war, Pir Vilayat pursued his spiritual training by studying with masters of many different religious traditions throughout India and the Middle East. While honoring the initiatic tradition of his predecessors, in his teachings Pir Vilayat continually adapted traditional Eastern spiritual practices in keeping with the evolution of Western consciousness. Throughout his life, he was an avid student of many religious and spiritual traditions and incorporated the rich mystical heritage of East and West into his teachings, adding to it the scholarship of the West in music, science, and psychology. He taught in the tradition of Universal Sufism, which views all religions as rays of light from the same sun.

Pir Vilayat initiated and participated in numerous international and interfaith conferences promoting understanding and world peace as well as convening spiritual and scientific leaders for public dialogues.

In 1975 he founded in the USA, the Abode of the Message, a central residential community of the Sufi Order International, a conference and retreat center, and a center of esoteric study. He also founded Omega Institute for Holistic Studies, a flourishing learning center, and published many books on aspects of meditation and realization.

Although travelling the world took up most of his time, Pir Vilayat continued to live in the family home, Fazl Manzil , in Suresnes, France. It is here that he build the L'Universel , a temple for all religions, in accordance to his father's inspiration.

In Europe he founded the "Summer Sufi Camps", yearly meditation camps high up in the Alps. He founded and inspired Zenith Institute, in Switzerland.

A Propos de l'Auteur

Pir Vilayat Inayat Khan (1916-2004) était le fils ainé et le successeur spirituel de Hazrat Pir O Murshid Inayat Khan, le premier maître soufi à enseigner en Occident. Pir Vilayat Inayat Khan est né Angleterre et a été élevé en France. Il a étudié à La Sorbonne, à Oxford et à l'Ecole Nationale de Musique de Paris. Pendant la deuxième guerre mondiale, il servit dans la Marine Royale Britannique (British Royal Navy) et il lui fut assigné le rôle de dragueur de mines, pendant l'invasion de la Normandie. Sa sœur, Noor Inayat Khan, servit dans la section française du SOE britannique (Special Operations Executive = Exécutif des Opérations Spéciales) comme opératrice à la radio. Elle fut capturée et exécutée en 1944 au camp de concentration de Dachau.

Après la guerre, Pir Vilayat poursuivit son entrainement spirituel avec des maîtres de différentes traditions religieuses, en Inde et au Moyen Orient. Tout en respectant la tradition initiatique de ses prédécesseurs dans son enseignement, Pir Vilayat adapta continuellement des pratiques spirituelles de la tradition orientale pour qu'elles soient en accord avec l'évolution de la pensée occidentale. Tout au long de sa vie, il fut avide d'étudier de nombreuses traditions religieuses et spirituelles et il incorpora le riche héritage mystique de l'Orient et de l'Occident dans ses enseignements, y ajoutant les savoirs de l'Occident dans la musique, la science et la psychologie. Il enseigna dans la tradition du soufisme universel qui considère toutes les religions comme des rayons de lumière d'un même soleil.

Pir Vilayat initia de nombreuses conférences interreligieuses internationales, auxquelles il participa, promouvant la compréhension et la paix mondiale et invitant des leaders spirituels et scientifiques à des dialogues publics.

En 1975, il fonda aux USA, « The Abode of the Message » (La Demeure du Message), une communauté résidentielle au sein de l'Ordre Soufi International, un centre pour les retraites et les conférences, ainsi que pour l'étude ésotérique. Il fonda aussi un centre florissant, l'Institut Omega pour les Etudes Holistiques, et publia de nombreux livres sur les aspects de la méditation et de la réalisation.

Bien que voyager autour du monde ait pris la plupart de son temps, Pir Vilayat continua à vivre dans la maison familiale, Fazl Manzil, à Suresnes, en France. C'est là qu'il a bâti l'Universel, un temple pour toutes les religions, en accord avec l'inspiration transmise par son père.

En Europe, il fonda les « Camps d'été Soufis » qui sont des camps de méditation perchés dans les Alpes, ayant lieu chaque année. Il fonda et inspira l'Institut Zénith, en Suisse.

Über den Autor

Pir Vilayat Inayat Khan (1916-2004) war der älteste Sohn und spiritueller Nachfolger von Hazrat Pir-O-Murshid Inayat Khan, dem ersten Sufimeister, der im Westen lehrte. Vilayat Inayat Khan wurde in England geboren und wuchs in Frankreich auf. Er studierte an der Sorbonne, in Oxford und an der École Normale de Musique de Paris. Im zweiten Weltkrieg diente er in der British Royal Navy und wurde bei den Minenräumarbeiten während der Invasion in die Normandie eingesetzt. Seine Schwester, Noor Inayat Khan, diente in der französischen Sektion der Britischen SOE (Special Operations Executive) als Funkerin. Sie wurde gefangen genommen und 1944 im Konzentrationslager Dachau hingerichtet.

Nach dem Krieg verfolgte Pir Vilayat seine spirituelle Ausbildung bei Meistern aus vielen verschiedenen religiösen Traditionen in Indien und im Mittleren Osten. Während er auf der einen Seite die Einweihungstradition seiner Vorgänger ehrte, passte Pir Vilayat auf der anderen Seite in seinen Lehren die traditionellen östlichen spirituellen Übungen kontinuierlich an die Entwicklung des westlichen Bewusstseins an. Sein ganzes Leben lang war er ein passionierter Schüler convieler Religionen und spiritueller Traditionen, und er verkörperte das reiche mystische Erbe von Ost und West in seinen Lehren, indem er ihnen die Gelehrsamkeit des Westens in Musik, Wissenschaft und Psychologie hinzufügte. Er lehrte in der Tradition des Universellen Sufismus, der alle Religionen als Lichtstrahlen aus der gleichen Sonne betrachtet.

Pir Vilayat initiierte und nahm Teil an zahlreichen internationalen und interreligiösen Konferenzen, um sowohl Verständnis und Weltfrieden unterstützen, als auch um führende spirituelle und wissenschaftliche Personen zum öffentlichen Dialog versammeln.

1975 gründete er in den USA die Abode of the Message, eine zentrale Lebens- und Wohngemeinschaft des Internationalen Sufiordens, ein Konferenz- und Retreatzentrum, und ein Zentrum für esoterische Studien. Auch gründete er das Omega Institut für ganzheitliche Studien, ein blühendes Lernzentrum, und er veröffentlichte viele Bücher über Aspekte der Meditation und Realisation.

Auch wenn er die meiste Zeit die Welt bereiste, so lebte er doch weiterhin im Heim der Familie in Fazl Manzil in Suresnes, Frankreich. Hier baute er in Übereinstimmung mit der Inspiration seines Vaters den Universel, einen Tempel für alle Religionen.

In Europa gründete er die „Sufi Sommercamps", jährliche Meditationscamps hoch oben in den Alpen. Er gründete und inspirierte Zenith Institute in der Schweiz.

more information in English:
Please visit
www.inayatiorder.org
www.sufiorderuk.org
www.zenithinstitute.com

weitere Information in Deutsch:
www.sufiorden.de
www.sufismus.ch
www.sufiorden.at
www.zenithinstitute.com/de/

plus d'informations en français:
www.ordre-soufi-international-france.org
www.zenithinstitute.com/fr/